MAKING SENSE OF YOUR LIFE'S JOURNEY

David S. Philemon

Royal Diadem Publishing Inc.

Dedication

To the Almighty God, my foundation and ever-present help. I am grateful for Your boundless love and grace that sustain me daily. And to my mentor in ministry, Rev. George Izunwa, whose steadfast commitment to the call of God has deeply impacted my life. Your guidance and support have been invaluable, encouraging me to walk boldly in the path God has set before me. Thank you for your example and your heart for the Kingdom

ACKNOWLEDGMENTS

This book would not have been possible without the unwavering support, dedication, and talent of an extraordinary team. My deepest gratitude goes to each of you for your contributions, insights, and encouragement throughout this journey.

First and foremost, thank you to Rev. Mimi Philemon my dear wife, Rev. Shina Gentry, and and my assistant pastor Rev. Bright Amudoaghan for your incredible effort, encouragement, and belief in this project. Your support has been instrumental in bringing this vision to life.

To the dedicated leaders of Royal Diadem Publishing, Ide Imogie and Kishawna Bailey, I am immensely grateful for your belief in this project from the very beginning and for investing your time and energy into its development. Your creativity, dedication, and expertise have been the backbone of this endeavor.

I am especially grateful to the Royal Diadem Publishing team—Beulah Orogun, Emmanuella Ben-Eboh, Doyinsade Awodele, Kim Matthews, and Shante Gill, for your meticulous attention to detail, refining every page and ensuring that each word reflects our vision.

A heartfelt thank you to my family, friends, and colleagues whose unwavering support and belief in this project gave me the courage and strength to see it through.

Finally, thank you to all the readers and supporters who make this work meaningful. I am humbled and honored to share this journey with each of you.

With all my gratitude,
David Philemon

CONTENTS

Title Page

Copyright

Dedication

Acknowledgments

Introduction   1

Part One: Foundation for Spiritual Growth   3

Chapter One   4

Chapter Two   11

Expecting Unusual Possibilities and Answers from the Third   12
Heaven (Part One)

Chapter Three   17

Extraordinary Miracles: All Round Sweetness (Part One)   18

Chapter Four   23

Extraordinary Miracles: All Round Sweetness (Part Two)   24

Chapter Five   29

Expecting Unusual Possibilities and Answers from The Third   30
Heaven (Part Two)

Chapter Six   34

All Round Sweetness and Special Miracles (Part Three)   35

Chapter Seven   40

Activating Your Week Through Prayer and Supernatural   41

Help

Chapter Eight   46

The Power of Words and Spiritual Warfare   47

Part Two: Deepening Your Spiritual Walk   52

Chapter Nine   53

Embracing the New Things God is Doing   54

Chapter Ten   58

Waiting on God's Timing   59

Chapter Eleven   64

Dedication to The Spirit   65

Chapter Twelve   70

Spiritual Protocols and Help   71

Chapter Thirteen   76

Battles and Deliverance   77

Chapter Fourteen   81

Commanding Supernatural Help   82

Chapter Fifteen   85

Mercy and the Blood of Jesus   86

Chapter Sixteen   90

The Wisdom of Prioritization in Our Lives   91

Conclusion   95

A SPECIAL CALL TO SALVATION & NEW BEGINNINGS FROM   97
APOSTLE DR. DAVID PHILEMON

INTRODUCTION

Making Sense Of Your Walk With
God In The Second Quarter

E very believer has a priceless opportunity to review, realign, and renew their lives and their walk with God, spiritual commitments, and dealings during the second quarter of this year.

It's a moment when faith, potent prayers, and obedience can eliminate the devil's write-ups. It's a chance to celebrate unusual testimonies alone and a time to activate God's promises of progress, peace, prosperity, and breakthrough.

In this phase of spiritual recalibrating, there's an important test: where do you put your trust? Is it using the chariots and horses of this world, or is it in the name of the Lord? Every believer is responsible for reaffirming their faith in God's omnipotence and providence. God frequently demands confidence from believers beyond pious words when they face life's hardships and challenges of daily existence.

God does not want our walk with Him to be shabby and plastic; rather, He desires that it be one of the best things that happen to us as we activate effective methods to demonstrate our faith in God.

Today, every believer must live in the same spirit as the ancient patriarchs.

When you place yourself in a position to make sense of your walk with God, you have chosen to hold on to the most crucial thing and grand in the scheme of eternity.

You have positioned yourself to neutralize Lukewarmness and push your attention to eternal things.

This is how to maximize eternal treasures. Imagine if the rich young ruler had followed Jesus—he would have gained much more than he ever had.

Don't you ever compare the desire for material gain to spiritual wealth? Don't you ever because this has led many believers astray.

God wants you to make sense of your walk with Him and accumulate a wealth of His fullness.

Don't neglect to study how to win souls for Christ. Don't neglect God's desires. Don't neglect your desires to seek to build God's kingdom. Don't neglect to hold onto things that will eternally satisfy you.

This is what the Lord wants to set the stage for in this spiritual book. As you trust God in this second quarter of the year for more profound dedication, spiritual insight, and divine support, may you never be disappointed.

PART ONE: FOUNDATION FOR SPIRITUAL GROWTH

CHAPTER ONE

ENFORCING GOD'S

SHINE FORTH AGENDA: STAND BOLD

A Week Of Unusual Possibilities

Are you anticipating what the Lord will do this week, beloved? This week presents numerous opportunities. As *"faith is the substance of things hoped for, the evidence of things not seen"* (Hebrews 11:1, KJV), let us approach this week with an expectant mindset, trusting that we will receive answers from the third heaven.

Our theme for this week is *"**Enforcing God's Shine Forth Agenda: Stand Bold**!"* You are part of a global movement that God is empowering. Let's align with His plan and eagerly anticipate amazing things from Him.

The Truth About Light And Darkness

You may have noticed the increasing focus on darkness around the globe. Stories of natural disasters, wars, economic downturns, and moral decline dominate the media. However, do not let appearances deceive you. The prevalence of darkness does not indicate its triumph. Light can instantly conquer darkness, whereas darkness cannot wholly extinguish light.

"The light shines in the darkness, and the darkness has not conquered it" (John 1:5, TLB). No matter how profound the darkness may seem in your life, family, or circumstances, it will dissipate as soon as God's light enters the picture.

Anticipate the remnants of darkness in your life to disappear as His light illuminates your path this week, a week of extraordinary possibilities. Declare this truth over your life: "In the name of Jesus, I will not fail; I will not be ashamed!"

God Of All Possibilities

God that we worship is an expert at the impossibly difficult. This is not feasible with men, but it is possible with God, according to Matthew 19:26 (AMPC). The ability of God to take circumstances that appear contradictory, unpleasant, or impossible and transform them into something beautiful is what we mean when we talk about possibilities.

It is possible to transform sorrow into joy, ashes into beauty, and dust into solid rock. Which scenario in your life does not seem conceivable right now? Remain assured that God has the power to change things. The things that confine us do not confine him. God of all possibilities, that is.

The Eye Of A Needle: A Test Of The Heart

Jesus explained this reality using the analogy of a rich man trying to enter the Kingdom of God. He said it was easier for a camel to go through the eye of a needle than for a rich person who trusts in wealth to enter the Kingdom. As explained historically, the eye of a needle refers to a small door in Israel. For a camel to go through it, it would have to strip off its baggage and lower itself. Likewise, no matter how wealthy or accomplished we are, we must be willing to strip off every reliance on earthly things and humbly submit ourselves to God's will.

This isn't about rejecting wealth but ensuring that nothing we possess controls us. Everything we own must be placed in God's hands for His glory and purposes. Wealth is not inherently evil, but it should not be allowed to dictate our priorities. Remember, God is the source of true satisfaction.

Desire For More: A God-Given Instinct

God instilled in humanity an innate desire for more. Following the fall of man, people attempted to satiate this longing with fleeting pursuits—wealth, power, fame, and momentary pleasures. However, only a deepening relationship with God and fulfilling His purpose can satisfy the void within.

A poignant illustration of this truth is the rich young ruler in *"Luke 18:18-30"* (TLB), who missed God's abundant blessings due to his reluctance to relinquish earthly possessions. Despite keeping all the commandments, he walked away sorrowfully when Jesus instructed him to sell his possessions and follow Him. He had everything yet lacked the essential element that would have infused his life with true meaning: wholehearted devotion to God's kingdom.

In the Kingdom of God, even possessing 99% is insufficient; the missing 1% often holds the key to unlocking God's full blessings.

Kingdom Dedication: The Missing Link

Many believers today are missing that vital 1%. We hold on to important things, but they are meaningless in the grand scheme of eternity. Satan often neutralizes Christians by making them lukewarm. He diverts our attention to material things, making us miss out on eternal treasures. Imagine if the rich young ruler had followed Jesus—he would have gained much more than he ever had.

Likewise, the desire for material gain has led many believers astray. We read books on accumulating wealth but neglect to study how to win souls for Christ. What are your desires? Are you seeking to build God's kingdom or holding onto things that will eventually desert you?

Aligning With God's Plan For Prosperity

Matthew 16:16-18 (TLB) reveals that Peter's confession of Christ as the Son of the living God was not a human revelation but one from the Spirit. Likewise, we must learn to walk in divine realities, not just humans. Satan wants us to operate within our human limits, but God calls us to higher realities where all things are possible.

God is not against your progress, prosperity, or success. Every sacrifice you make for the sake of His Kingdom will come back to you multiplied. The most blessed position you can be in is in the center of God's will. When you and your family are aligned with His purpose, you will experience unprecedented favor and breakthroughs.

The Power Of Revelation And Obedience

God constantly releases revelations to His people, but every revelation comes with instructions. It is not enough to hear from God; we must act on what we have heard. David heard from God and followed divine desires, and within 13 years, he was sitting on the throne of Israel.

How often have we heard from God but failed to act because

we didn't fully trust Him or because the instruction seemed too complicated? Many Christians cannot experience the fullness of God's prosperity because they struggle with obedience. However, we will unlock unusual possibilities as we follow God's instructions.

The God Of Unusual Possibilities

Throughout Scripture, we see examples of God performing what seemed impossible. John 9:31-32 (TPT) reminds us that God hears the prayers of those who worship Him and do His will. This week, get ready to see unusual possibilities manifest in your life. Just as God opened blind eyes, healed the sick, and raised the dead, He will perform miraculous wonders in your life. Get ready for the God of all possibilities to move in ways you've never imagined.

God Will Heal And Restore

Some of you have been praying for breakthroughs in your health, finances, relationships, or ministry. This week, I believe God will heal ears, open eyes, and perform unbelievable miracles. The same power that raised Jesus from the dead will be displayed in your life.

Walk In Boldness And Expectation

As we close, let me remind you that the dimension of God's power you walk in is determined by the sacrifices you are willing to make. God has already given you access to divine possibilities, but it's up to you to respond in faith and obedience.

Stand bold this week! Expect unusual possibilities, and

enter the complete revelation of who you are in Christ. As you do, the light of God will shine forth in your life, dispelling all traces of darkness and glorifying His name in all you do. **You are called to a life of celebration, not devastation.**

Declare it: I am aligned with God's Shine Forth Agenda! I will stand bold and expect unusual possibilities in my life this week, in Jesus' name. Amen.

CHAPTER TWO

EXPECTING UNUSUAL POSSIBILITIES AND ANSWERS FROM THE THIRD HEAVEN (PART ONE)

O pening Scripture: Proverbs 13:12 (KJV): "Hope deferred makes the heart sick: but when the desire comes, it is a tree of life."

If you believe this week is a time to anticipate extraordinary opportunities and responses from the Third Heaven. We are about to make a breakthrough, but it will need close consideration of spiritual precepts. As we explore this chapter, there are five main issues that we must deal with today: two that, if left unattended, will impede your destiny, and three that are necessary for God's promises to be fulfilled in your life. If you can grasp these ideas, you'll be ready for divine manifestation this week.

1. The Power of Moments:

Our first point highlights how important it is to honor moments. A lot of people don't realize how valuable time is. But in God's plan, every second, minute, hour, and day counts. The primary

Bible events—like Pentecost, which occurred at a precise, divinely scheduled time—prove this. Although the Holy Spirit arrived at the scheduled time, He did not immediately follow Jesus' ascension. Moments are, therefore, crucial to fate. It's risky to treat the moments that God offers you with disrespect.

Key Verse: Acts 2:1-4 (Pentecost happened at an appointed moment).

Just as seasons impact trees and their fruit-bearing potential, moments impact your life's outcome. Harsh winters may seem to kill the tree, but when spring comes, the tree flourishes again. Likewise, in your spiritual journey, difficult moments may seem to dry up your potential but expect God's seasons of revival. As we align with God's timing this week, expect supernatural possibilities.

2. The Weight of Patterns and Cycles:

Destinies often fail because of repeated failures. When failure becomes a pattern, it appears to be an insurmountable mountain. The Bible reminds us that "*hope deferred makes the heart sick*" (Proverbs 13:12). Failures can crush hope when they become patterns. However, the pattern is stronger than the demon trying to stop you. A bad season doesn't mean it's over. Spring is coming!

Consider trees again: a tree produces fruit in seasons following a pattern. When you plant a tree, you don't keep replanting it; it follows its God-ordained cycle. Your life is the same—when you follow God's pattern, you will bear fruit in your due season.

Key Lesson: The fruit is the outcome, but the tree is the pattern. Pay attention to the patterns in your life as they determine your harvest.

3. Relationships: The Trees of Life:

Relationships are like trees. Satan fights fruitful relationships, especially spiritual ones. When you are connected to a relationship that bears fruit in your life—whether it's a prayer partner, mentor, or spiritual covering—Satan will do everything to sabotage it. Why? Because flourishing relationships produce fruit that glorifies God.

Satan fertilizes false relationships that yield sour fruit, but God blesses the proper connections in your life. If you have a genuine prayer partner or spiritual covering, cherish and nurture those relationships. These relationships are vital to your spiritual growth, and the enemy knows that disconnecting you from them can halt your progress.

Key Lesson: When you find a God-ordained relationship, stay connected. Don't allow Satan to frustrate or sabotage what God has planted in your life.

4. The Importance of Spiritual Covering:

It is dangerous to live without spiritual covering. In 2 Kings 5, Naaman almost misses his miracle because of pride and anger. He expected Elisha to come out and heal him, but instead, Elisha sent a simple instruction: "Go wash in the Jordan seven times." Naaman's initial reaction was offense. However, once he obeyed, his healing came.

Satan loves to make you feel like you don't need spiritual covering. He fosters offenses and pride to separate you from your God-appointed leadership. But every believer needs spiritual guidance —a covering that keeps you accountable, sharpens you, and helps you grow in wisdom.

Key Lesson: Your spiritual covering is vital. Don't let pride, offenses, or instability disorganize your life and disconnect you from those God has placed over you.

5. Nature Versus Nurture in Spiritual Growth:

Some people are naturally inclined to specific behaviors—whether good or bad. However, even naturally gifted people must be nurtured and trained to develop their potential. This applies to our spiritual walk as well. You may be naturally talented in certain areas, but those gifts will never reach their full potential without discipline and training.

In the same way, you may struggle in areas where you are not naturally inclined. However, with intentional effort and nurturing the Holy Spirit, even the things that don't come quickly to you can be developed.

Key Lesson: What God has placed in you will be sharpened as you train it. Even the areas you struggle with can grow if you intentionally nurture them.

Spiritual Adoption:

As we consider our adoption into God's family (Ephesians 1:5), we see that just as adopted children often carry the traits of their biological parents, we have the traits of our heavenly Father. But for those traits to fully manifest, we must embrace our identity in Christ and submit to His nurturing process. After his healing, Naaman embraced his role as a worshiper of God, signifying his acceptance of sonship.

Key Lesson: Your adoption into God's family is a powerful spiritual reality. Embrace the identity and nurture that comes with it.

This week, we are stepping into unusual possibilities and answers from the Third Heaven. But it is crucial to pay attention to the spiritual principles we have discussed:

1. *Respect the power of moments*—every second counts in God's plan.

2. **Recognize and break negative patterns**—don't let repeated failures define your destiny.

3. **Cherish fruitful relationships**—Satan will fight them, but God will bless them.

4. **Submit to spiritual covering**—your protection and growth depend on it.

5. **Embrace the nurturing process**—whether through natural gifts or intentional growth, God's work in you is ongoing.

As you align with these principles, expect this week to be one of breakthrough, manifestation, and answered prayers from the

Third Heaven. Amen!

Prayer

Heavenly Father, we thank You for the revelation of Your word. As we step into this week of unusual possibilities, we ask for Your grace to master the principles aligning us with Your divine will. Help us to honor the moments You give us, to break free from negative patterns, and to cherish the relationships You have blessed us with. Keep us under Your spiritual covering, and nurture us into the fullness of what You have called us to be. We declare this week will be a week of answers and breakthroughs in Jesus' mighty name. Amen!

CHAPTER THREE

EXTRAORDINARY MIRACLES: ALL ROUND SWEETNESS (PART ONE)

I t's critical to acknowledge the spiritual importance of making the correct decisions in life as we start this week of extraordinary miracles. God wants us to act with faith when He is in our lives and wait on Him in prayer. Prayer and action must go hand in hand with believers, and we must believe that God will support us when we take risks. This week, we'll examine how God is calling us to proceed while having faith that He will do miracles in many spheres of our lives, including relationships, finances, spirituals, and more.

Foundation Scripture: Exodus 14:13-15 (KJV, ERV)

The Red Sea tale of Moses is a potent reminder of the need for faith and action. Moses called out to God for assistance when the Egyptian army had trapped the Israelites. But God's answer caught them off guard: "Why are you calling out to me? Give the Israelites the order to proceed. (Exodus 14:15, ERV)

God wants us to do more than just pray; He wants us to take decisive action. Although prayer is essential, it needs to be combined with action. Even though Moses knew God would act,

God required the Israelites to act with faith.

The Power of Humility and Submission

Being God's children, we must learn humility and submit our opinions to His. Proverbs 3:5–6 says, "In all your ways, submit to the Lord, and He will make your paths straight; trust in the Lord with all your heart and lean not on your understanding."

We should listen to God's voice and seek His guidance in our decisions. His heart sings when He is acknowledged because it demonstrates faith. Like Moses, we frequently have faith that God will act, but we still have to do our part to bring about that miracle. Recognizing God's plan and following His guidance are the keys to experiencing unique miracles.

Action Brings Miracles

The miracle at the Red Sea did not happen until Moses stretched out his hand over the water. Likewise, we all have something God can use to perform a miracle. It could be a talent, an idea, or an opportunity we need to act on. As believers, we must learn that every revelation from God must be attached to an action to birth a revolution.

James 2:17 says, *"Faith without works is dead."* When we pray and receive direction from God, we must act on it. This is how we birth extraordinary miracles. If 100,000 Christians across the globe made a move towards studying cybersecurity, technology, or another area, think of the impact! Yet, often, we wait too long instead of taking the necessary steps.

God Loves Movers:

God is the God of action. He moves with those who are ready to move. Isaiah 40:31 (ERV) declares, *"But those who trust the Lord will find new strength. They will soar high on wings like eagles. They will run and not grow weary. They will walk and not faint."*

When we trust in God's strength, we become movers and doers. There are different seasons in life—somewhere we are called to fly, others where we are called to run, and somewhere we are required to walk. Regardless of the season, we must never be stagnant. God expects His children to be people of motion.

Special Moves Lead to Special Miracles

One key point is that **extraordinary miracles come to those who make special moves**. In John 2:7-8, Jesus instructed the servants to fill the waterpots with water, and as they obeyed, the water turned into wine. Mary prayed, the disciples moved, and the guests enjoyed the miracle. Notice how their obedience to a simple instruction led to an extraordinary result.

Have you been praying and waiting for a miracle? This week, God is calling you to make a move. Praying alone is not enough; we must also act on the revelations we receive in prayer. God will not do what He expects us to do for ourselves.

Build Wealth with Wisdom

When God gives us resources—whether financial, intellectual, or relational—He expects us to steward them wisely. Building wealth in the Kingdom requires strategic moves. Start with minimum risk for medium profit, and as you accumulate profit, reinvest it. Never risk your capital on maximum-risk ventures. This principle applies not just to finances but to every area of life.

Proverbs 21:5 says, *"The plans of the diligent lead to profit as surely as haste leads to poverty."* Diligence and careful planning will lead to long-term success. When you apply these principles consistently, you build something solid that can withstand any storm.

Never Downgrade Yourself

Sometimes in life, we face trials, tribulations, or situations that make us tired and tempted to give up. However, **it is essential never to downgrade yourself** because of your circumstances. God never downgrades His children. If you find yourself tired, do not ask for the grace to crawl—ask for the grace to stand.

The enemy would love for you to slow down or stop altogether, but God calls us to keep moving forward. Philippians 3:14

encourages us to *"press on toward the goal to win the prize for which God has called [us] heavenward in Christ Jesus."* If you are tired, ask God for strength to continue moving, and He will provide it.

The Church as the Solution

Today's world is looking for solutions, and many of those solutions are supposed to come from the Church. The miracle will not come from outside the Church but from within. We, as believers, are called to be lenders, not borrowers (Deuteronomy 28:12). We are the ones to create solutions in areas such as business, technology, government, education, and more.

God has been preparing a tribe of people in secret, and now it is time for them to rise and take their place in the world. God has trained some of you for years and has given you wings to fly. It is time to stop walking and start soaring.

Moving Beyond Comfort

Too often, believers remain comfortable where they are. But to see extraordinary miracles, we must push beyond our comfort zones. If you have been walking, it's time to start running. If you have been running, it's time to start flying. Do not be satisfied with small achievements when God has called you to more incredible things.

God is not limited by what seems impossible to us. He is the God of all possibilities. He wants to see His children thriving in every area of life. The goal is to succeed financially and build wealth that multiplies and impacts others.

Rewarding Yourself

Learn to reward yourself as you begin to make moves and see progress. There is power in delayed gratification, but it is also important to celebrate the small wins. Find ways to reward yourself that align with your goals and bring fulfillment. This could be through personal development, investing in your health, or even taking time to rest and rejuvenate.

This week is a special week of miracles, but those miracles will only manifest when we make special moves. God has already instructed us to move forward, just as He did with Moses at the Red Sea. Now, it is up to us to take action.

Let this be the week where you stop crawling and start walking, where you stop walking and start running, and where you stop running and start flying. God has given you everything you need to succeed, but it's up to you to take the steps to activate the miracle.

Are you ready to see extraordinary miracles in your life? Then make the move God calls you to, and watch Him do the impossible.

CHAPTER FOUR

EXTRAORDINARY MIRACLES: ALL ROUND SWEETNESS (PART TWO)

"God was performing extraordinary miracles by the hands of Paul" - Acts 19:11 (KJV).

"You prepare a table before me in the presence of my enemies; You anoint my head with oil; my cup overflows." Psalm 23:5

It has been declared that this week will be marked by extraordinary miracles—miracles beyond the norm. God wants to unleash His dunamis, or power to accomplish miracles, rather than only bestowing upon us material blessings. We will delve into the extent of God's specific favoritism toward His people today and discover how we are set up for overall sweetness in our lives.

1. The Reality of Special Miracles

Acts 19:11 speaks of "special miracles" that God performed through the hands of Paul. It is crucial to understand that these miracles were **extraordinary**, beyond the everyday workings of grace we are used to seeing. Extraordinary miracles go beyond everyday experiences—they defy human understanding and natural laws.

Some things should happen to others but should never happen to you as a child of God. Why? Because you belong to a class by yourself—a class marked by the favor and anointing of God. On the other hand, some blessings that do not occur to others should happen to you simply because of God's preferential treatment of His beloved.

This kind of preferential treatment is the foundation for **extraordinary miracles**. God works uniquely in your life to display His glory. He causes you to stand out as a reflection of His power and might, giving you testimonies that will advertise His special grace.

2. The Source of Special Miracles: Dunamis Power

The Greek word for extraordinary miracles is **dunamis**, meaning explosive, dynamic power—power that produces results. It is not just any power but God's **miracle-working ability**. This is the same power that raised Jesus from the dead, opened the eyes of the blind, and empowered Paul to perform miraculous signs and wonders.

This dunamis power is what sets you apart. When God releases it over your life, you begin to operate in supernatural realms, doing what would be impossible without His intervention. Psalm 23:5 says, "*You anoint my head with oil; my cup overflows.*" This overflowing anointing comes from the presence of God's dunamis in your life. You carry a spiritual dynamite that makes every area of your life explode with goodness, favor, and divine attention.

3. A Life of Overflow

When God places His hand on you, it becomes impossible for you to be dry. Just as a pipe that carries water cannot remain dry, a person connected to God's dunamis cannot stay without results. Your blessings are not just for you; they overflow to others.

Genesis 12:2-3 tells us that God promised Abraham, "*I will make of you a great nation, and I will bless you, and make your name great; and you shall be a blessing."* The same applies to us today—God blesses us so that we may become a blessing to others. Your overflow is not just for you to enjoy but for others to partake in. People who come into contact with you will be impacted by the power of God that flows through you, just as the people around Paul experienced God's miracles.

4. The Promise of Greater Glory

As wonderful as the miracles we have seen are, God promises even greater things. The signs and wonders we witness today are just the beginning. The former and latter rains are our portion, but we have yet to scratch the surface of what God has in store for His people.

In 1 Kings 4:20-28, God gave King Solomon wisdom beyond human understanding. Even prostitutes—those least expected—were used to announce the king's wisdom. Similarly, God wants to use your life to reflect His wisdom and power, even in unexpected situations.

When God raises you, it is not for your glory but for His. His miracles in your life will become a testimony to those around you, even in complex and challenging situations. Elisha performed magnificent acts, Elijah performed mighty acts, and you are called to experience even more incredible things through the power of the Holy Spirit.

5. The Role of Humility and Discipline

However, humility is essential for God to continue working in your life. When God raises you, He also disciplines you. Proverbs 3:12 reminds us, *"whom the Lord loves, He corrects."* Discipline, punctuality, and humility are keys to sustaining the flow of God's extraordinary miracles in your life.

Humility opens the door for you to receive more of God's wisdom. When God corrects you, do not resist; embrace the lessons He is teaching you. Be punctual in your assignments, and do not compare yourself to others. Don't try to be a fork if God has called you a spoon. Serve in the capacity He has called you and will overflow your life.

6. The Impact of Special Miracles on Your Generation

God's extraordinary miracles in your life are not just for you—they are meant to impact your generation. Acts 19:11-12 says, *"God did extraordinary miracles through Paul, so that even handkerchiefs and aprons that had touched him were taken to the sick, and their illnesses were cured, and the evil spirits left them."*

Your life is meant to be a conduit of God's power to those around you. Your overflow will become a source of blessing to multitudes. The extraordinary miracles in your life will cause others to experience the greatness of God.

As we end, remember that we worship a God of unique miracles who longs to infuse our lives with a general sweetness. You have access to the dunamis power that was upon Paul right now. It's time to step into that power and use it to channel God's grace, favor, and mighty acts.

Prayers

1. Father, in the name of Jesus, by Your power and authority, thank You for hearing and answering our prayers. Take all the glory and praise in Jesus' name.

2. Father, in the name of Jesus, I receive Your wisdom, favor, and extraordinary miracles in my life. Let my life overflow with special attention from heaven.

3. Father, in the name of Jesus, I declare that the dunamis of God is upon me. I receive miracle-working ability, explosiveness, and divine overflow. Let my life reflect Your glory in every area.

May the Lord continue to shower you with His extraordinary miracles, and may your life be a reflection of His power in this week of all-round sweetness, in Jesus' name. Amen.

CHAPTER FIVE

EXPECTING UNUSUAL POSSIBILITIES AND ANSWERS FROM THE THIRD HEAVEN (PART TWO)

A s we explore our purpose and destiny, let us remember that this is not only an individual journey but also a group one intricately linked to the lives of people around us. Our responsibilities are to God, who has predetermined our pathways, ourselves, and others we are supposed to uplift.

The Call to Connection

Not only is the history of Jesus' twelfth-year journey a historical one, but it also offers a potent allegory for our own experiences. We, too, need to look for the locations, people, and ideas that firmly establish our divine calling, just as Jesus was found in the temple, having conversations that shaped His sense of mission. Luke 2:48–50 TPT serves as a reminder that even though people might not always see our value or calling, we must not give up on the dreams that God has given us.

We have to face Satan's diversionary tactics in this endeavor as well. He wants to cut us from everything, including our communities, spiritual teachers, and purpose. These relationships serve as lifelines, guiding us through the rough seas of life. We run the risk of straying from our desired course without them.

Accepting Responsibility

We must take ownership of our spiritual development. This entails actively participating in the process of identifying who our spiritual covering is, not just admitting our shortcomings and errors. This covering serves as both a nurturer and a protector, pushing us to become the people we were meant to be and supporting our personal development. Hebrews 12:2 TPT encourages us to focus on Jesus as our faith's creator and consummate figure.

We will remain rooted if we can identify the voices that matter in our lives—sincere and encouraging. Instead of people who want to appease you, surround yourself with people who help you pursue your purpose. Relationships need discernment because not everyone we meet claims to be supportive and genuinely wants what's best for us.

The Dangers of Poor Connections

We come against the perils of bad connections as we travel toward our destiny. Having a prayer companion is beneficial, but we need to exercise caution. Do they want to help you, or are they just curious about what you can do for them? *"Whoever walks with the wise becomes wise, but the companion of fools will suffer harm,"* according to Proverbs 13:20. Make thoughtful partner selections.

We risk stagnating when we lower our guard and invite sycophants who only tell us what we want to hear into our inner circle. The voices in our environment ought to push us, demand accountability from us, and inspire us to advance. We can tell when we are among faithful destiny helpers because they will motivate us to pursue God's plan with vigor and passion.

The Process of Transformation

The transformation of our lives is often a gradual process, much like the dismantling of rocks that have become entrenched in our lives. Matthew 15:30-31 TPT depicts how Jesus healed the sick and transformed lives, and it is a reminder that we, too, are called to be agents of transformation. We must not fear confronting the "rocks" formed through years of neglect or poor choices. This may require time, effort, and God's divine intervention, but it is essential for our growth.

Embracing Unusual Possibilities

We unlock unusual possibilities by aligning ourselves with God's purpose and the right people. The power of God is transformative; it can change our lives and those around us. 2 Peter 1:3-4 TPT assures us that through His divine power, we have everything we need for a godly life. This is a call to embrace the life that God has designed for us—a life where we are partakers of His divine nature and all the possibilities that come with it.

We become vessels of unusual possibilities when we cultivate our connection with God and those He places in our lives. We can witness miracles unfold in our lives and the lives of others. Luke 5:26 TPT, KJV celebrates the amazement of those who witnessed the miracles Jesus performed, proclaiming, "We have seen strange things today!" May our lives reflect that same wonder, glorifying God in every aspect.

Prophetic Encouragement

As we draw this message close, let's reflect on the incredible journey ahead. God has given us gifts, opportunities, and connections for a reason. Do not overlook the significance of your spiritual covering and the importance of surrounding yourself with destiny helpers.

Remember, God is constantly calling your heart, spirit, and soul to intimacy with Him. There is so much more ahead—unusual possibilities await you.

In the name of Jesus, I declare that each of you will discover your purpose and connect with the right people who will help you fulfill that purpose. You will rise to new heights, and as you do, others will celebrate the goodness of God in your life. Incredible! Amazing! This is God! May the Lord bless, protect, and guide you as you enter your divine destiny. Amen

CHAPTER SIX

ALL ROUND SWEETNESS AND SPECIAL MIRACLES (PART THREE)

There is a God skilled at raising His people and directing their ascent in a way that ensures their prosperity and never becomes an embarrassment. God ensures that the blessings He bestows upon us mature and last according to His flawless plan. He takes great pleasure in assembling the elements to bring about the lovely existence He has planned for us. In contrast, the enemy, Satan, works ceaselessly to transform beauty into ashes. He wants to ruin what God has created so exquisitely, but His work is always restoration, transforming ashes into beauty.

According to Isaiah 61:3, God provides us "beauty for ashes," a promise that even in our darkest hours, God can transform our lives into something glorious.

Ashes to Beauty: A Divine Process

Turning ashes into beauty is not an instantaneous event; it requires the hand of God. Ashes are often the product of something that has been ruined, destroyed, or consumed by fire. In life, there are moments when we look at certain situations, and they seem beyond repair as if nothing good could ever come from them. But the good news is that God specializes in restoring even the most hopeless situations.

Consider how we often use the phrase "ashes to ashes, dust to dust" during burial ceremonies, signifying finality and death. However, God reverses the narrative. While Satan may rejoice in destruction, God turns what is broken into beauty.

The Enemy's Tactics

Satan, who was once the epitome of beauty (Ezekiel 28:13), understands the power of beauty, but his fallen nature cannot create or sustain it. Instead, he operates in a mindset of destruction, constantly seeking to ruin anything that reflects God's glory. This is evident in his attempts to manipulate and distort God's creation.

For example, in the story of a man who told his children they would never be more significant than him, we see the manifestation of this destructive mentality. The man's words were rooted in insecurity and the fallen nature, which mirrors Satan's desire to limit growth and beauty in others. However, through their connection to Christ, those children defied the limiting words spoken to them. God's intervention allowed them to rise above the negative pronouncement and become 100 times greater than their father.

Words Have Power

This leads us to an important truth: words never die but can be reversed. The Bible says that death and life are in the power of the tongue (Proverbs 18:21). Negative words spoken over your life can be canceled through prayer, faith, and God's power.

The Lord revealed through His servant that these children, who had surpassed their father, were being prepared for greater heights. Yet, a voice from their past was still waiting to try to bring them down. God instructed these children to fast and offer gifts to their father, even though he didn't deserve them, as a sign of humility and honor. In doing so, they would destroy the negative voice that once sought to limit their greatness.

Similarly, there may be voices waiting in your future, trying to bring you down as you rise into your destiny. Today, in the name of Jesus, every voice speaking against your progress, beauty, and glory will evaporate! The Lord prepares to destroy any voice that says you will never be beautiful and succeed. Beauty is not just physical appearance; it's the glory and signature of God upon your life.

Beauty as God's Signature

When the Bible speaks of beauty, it goes beyond outward appearances. Beauty represents God's glory, manifesting His works in your life. As God turns your ashes into beauty, your potential will come alive, and your purpose will be fulfilled.

Consider Philip from the Book of Acts. He was initially tasked with distributing food to the widows—a humble job that required faithfulness. Yet, because of his faithfulness in the "kitchen," God promoted him to a more excellent assignment. Philip became an evangelist to Samaria, performing miracles and spreading the gospel. God rewards faithfulness and uses our present circumstances as training grounds for the more significant tasks ahead. Many of you are in your own "kitchens" right now, where God is preparing you for greater responsibilities and miracles.

The Power of Faithfulness

God will often test us in small things before releasing us into our destiny. If we are faithful in little, God will make us rulers over much (Luke 16:10). Stephen, one of the seven chosen to serve food, was later martyred for his faith. Even in his death, his faithfulness and sacrifice spoke volumes, and his story continues to inspire the church.

You may be in a season of preparation right now, serving in what seems like a small or insignificant capacity. But remember, God is watching your faithfulness. He is preparing to release you into a season of extraordinary miracles, where your beauty—His glory in you—will shine forth for the world to see.

Satan's Attack on Your Destiny

As you rise into your purpose, know that Satan will attempt to fast forward any negative prophecy or proclamation spoken over your life. But those enemy plans can and will be canceled in Jesus' name. Every seed of destruction the enemy has planted will be uprooted, and every voice speaking against your destiny will be silenced.

In Acts 12:1-2, we read about the persecution of the early church. Herod killed James, while John survived multiple attempts on his life. The difference between James and John wasn't that John was more righteous or had more favor. Instead, John had a greater revelation of God's plan for his life, which protected him from destruction. In the same way, your portion in life is determined by your revelation of God's word and His promises for you. With this revelation, you will overcome every challenge and rise to the fullness of God's beauty in your life.

Only God is capable of orchestrating the magnificent metamorphosis from ashes to beauty. Trials and tribulations may accompany the trip, but the reward is always excellent. God is preparing you for a time of unique wonders and general pleasure. For His glory, He is mending what has been torn apart and transforming every wreck into a work of art.

You will see God's beauty fully shown in your life if you put your faith in Him, obey Him in the little things, and ignore any voice that tells you otherwise. In the name of Jesus, announce today that every ash in your life will be turned into beauty and that every barrier will be removed. You're meant to be great, and there's no stopping you. The past or future cannot stop the plans of God for your life. Your beauty—God's glory in you—will shine for the world.

Prayer

Heavenly Father, in the name of Jesus, we thank You for

Your faithfulness, kindness, and mercy. We stand in awe of Your power to turn ashes into beauty and bring sweetness into every area of our lives. Today, we ask that You silence every voice that seeks to limit our destiny. Let every plan of the enemy be destroyed, and may Your glory shine in and through us. In Jesus' name, Amen.

CHAPTER SEVEN

ACTIVATING YOUR WEEK THROUGH PRAYER AND SUPERNATURAL HELP

The focus of this chapter: This week is activated by my cry for a Father's help and supernatural response from Heaven.

As we consider this chapter, brothers, and sisters, I desire to say that this week is not just another week; it is a week loaded with divine possibilities, a week where God is ready to perfect things in our lives. Today, I want us to focus on activating our week by crying out for the Father's help and expecting a supernatural response from Heaven. God is our Father, and just as a loving father helps his children in times of need, God is ready to respond when we call on Him.

The Importance of Daily Connection with God

One of the most crucial things you can ever realize is that just as you need to breathe daily to stay alive physically, you need to connect with God daily to stay alive spiritually.

Many people reach a point in their spiritual journey where they feel like they have been praying for so long and grow weary. But think about it—no one says, "I've been breathing and breathing, and now I'm tired of breathing." The fact that you are breathing means you are alive, and if you want to stay alive, you must continue to breathe.

Similarly, your connection with God is your spiritual breath. If you are saved, you need the Holy Spirit every day, for He is the one who communicates the fullness of Christ to your body, spirit, and soul. Without this connection, your spirit cannot thrive, and your soul becomes weary. Your body also needs the power of God to remain solid and stable on this earth.

The Role of the Holy Spirit

The Holy Spirit is not just a distant concept; He is the communicator and transmitter of all God's fullness to humanity. When you pray, you express humility and acknowledge your dependence on God. You say, "Lord, I cannot make it alone." Every time you pray, you align your spirit with Heaven's agenda.

Prayer is not a ritual; it is your lifeline. It's how you engage with the supernatural. And when you activate your day or week through prayer, you partner with God, positioning yourself to receive His help. You are speaking life into your day and your week, just as God instructed Ezekiel to prophesy to the dry bones in Ezekiel 37. When discussing life, the Spirit of God breathes into our situations.

The Consequences of Spiritual Neglect

Now, let me tell you this: if you are tired of speaking life, the natural outcome is that weeds will grow. You can never be neutral. Even when things seem stagnant, something always happens in the spiritual realm. Jesus warned us in Matthew 13:3-6, saying that seeds sown on rocky or thorny ground will be choked by weeds if not nurtured properly.

When you pray, you ensure you have a say in how your day or week unfolds. If you don't speak over your life, Satan has already packaged evil plans for you. That is why Jesus taught us to pray, *"Lead us not into temptation, but deliver us from evil"* (Matthew 6:13). Every day, we face spiritual battles, and prayer is how we declare victory over those battles.

Daily Activation and Fertilization

When you activate your week through prayer, that's only the beginning. A week that is activated must be fertilized daily. Every prayer you pray is like water on the seeds you've planted. Over time, as you consistently invest in your spiritual life, your spiritual field becomes a "weed-killer." The weeds—the evil plans of the enemy—will die before they even have a chance to germinate.

In the realm of the spirit, fire represents power. The more you pray, the more spiritually fiery you become. And as Hebrews 12:29 tells us, *"Our God is a consuming fire."* Fire consumes, burns, and purifies. When you are on fire for God, no weapon formed against you can prosper (Isaiah 54:17). Evil cannot thrive in your life because the heat of your spiritual life scorches every plot and plan of the enemy.

Praying into the Future

Another critical aspect of prayer is that it allows you to send protection ahead of you. You don't have to wait for evil to strike before you pray. Prayer is proactive. The more you pray, the further away evil is from you. You can send prayers into your future to safeguard your family, health, finances, and every area of your life.

Isaiah 54:14 declares, *"In righteousness, you shall be established; you shall be far from oppression, for you shall not fear; and from terror, for it shall not come near you."* This promise becomes real when you invest in your spiritual life daily, sincerely, and passionately.

The Impact of Persistent Prayer

When you build a consistent prayer life, your life becomes a hostile environment for evil to thrive. When the enemy tries to plant sickness, fear, or destruction in your life, the fire of your prayers scorches those seeds before they can take root. In Psalm 3:2-4 (AMPC), the Bible says, *"Many are saying of me, 'God will not deliver him.' But You, O Lord, are a shield around me, my glory, the One who lifts my head high."*

People may say all kinds of things about you. They may have negative expectations, but what matters is what you say. Your words carry power. Proverbs 18:21 says, *"Death and life are in the power of the tongue."* Instead of sitting down and worrying about what others say, counter their words with God's promises. No one can bury you with their words if you refuse to give your consent.

Your Voice Matters

It's important to realize that your voice matters as much as others may pray for you. Your voice in prayer activates God's power in your life. Don't ever underestimate the power of your declarations. This is your week of saying! This is your week of speaking life over your circumstances.

Psalm 3:3 reminds us to declare:

1. **You are my shield** – God protects you from all harm.

2. **You are my glory** – God is the one who gives you honor and victory.

3. **You are the lifter of my head** – God restores your joy and dignity.

God steps into your situation with supernatural help as you declare these truths. Get ready for a Father's help—a help that is unconditional, solid, and powerful. When you cry out to your Father, He responds with the full force of Heaven.

Prayers For This Week

Let us take a moment to pray together as we activate this week.

Prayer One

Father, in Jesus's name, we thank You for Your power,

authority, grace, and mercy. Thank You for hearing our prayers and for endowing us with divine wisdom. We rely on You as our faithful God, who never fails. We thank You for Your kindness, for the gift of life, health, strength, and a sound mind. Thank You for the Holy Spirit, who empowers us daily. Take all the praise, Lord!

Prayer Two

Father, we declare this week that You are our shield, our glory, and the lifter of our heads. No weapon formed against us shall prosper. We activate this week with our words of faith, knowing that Your supernatural help is coming. We speak life, victory, and favor over every day this week. In Jesus' name, Amen!

Beloved, as we step into this new week, let us remember the power of activating our days through prayer. Don't wait for trouble to come before you pray; send prayers ahead of you. This week is a week of saying, a week of speaking life, and a week of receiving supernatural help from our Heavenly Father. Amen!

CHAPTER EIGHT

THE POWER OF
WORDS AND
SPIRITUAL WARFARE

"**M**any are saying of me, 'God will not deliver him.' But You, O Lord, are a shield around me, my glory, the One who lifts my head high." Psalm 3:2 (TPT, AMPC)

There is much power in words in this world. Both the words we speak and the words that are spoken over us have spiritual and practical consequences. Words can bless or damage, mold our future, direct our behavior, and impact our spiritual environment. Psalm 3 records David's prayer to God while foes encircled him. Despite their depressing remarks, David acknowledged the Lord as his glory and shield.

We will discuss the significance of comprehending the power of words, the spiritual warfare surrounding them, and how the Bible can help believers overcome the destructive words spoken over their lives.

1. *The Influence of Words*

Words are spiritual powers that can influence our world; they are more than just sounds. Proverbs 18:21 (KJV) reminds us that "death and life are in the power of the tongue, and they that love it shall eat the fruit thereof." This implies that our words and comments about us can bring about life or death.

A. The Power of Words Spoken Over Us

Negative Words: **People don't always speak just because you say nothing.** People frequently use words of discouragement, negativity, or even curses when speaking negatively about you. Things said out of resentment or rage can stay in the air and affect your life.

Positive Words: Conversely, some people speak blessings over your life. They declare that you are blessed, favored, a shining star, and destined to succeed. These words have power, too. They reinforce God's will for your life when aligned with God's Word.

When words of blessing or curses are left unchecked, they have the potential to manifest. As believers, we must be conscious of both the words spoken over us and the words we speak.

B. Prophecy of Words

Negative remarks made about you have the potential to become personal predictions if they are not refuted. God is your shield, even though others may doubt your deliverance, much like David in Psalm 3. By praying and confessing God's Word, we must develop the ability to withstand hurtful remarks.

2. David's Response to Negative Words

David faced many words of discouragement throughout his life. When King Saul sought to kill him, people may have spoken of David's downfall, but he never allowed those words to take root in his spirit.

A. The Story of Saul and David

Saul's jealousy led him to pursue David relentlessly. But even in the face of danger, David declared that it would not be by his hand that Saul would die. Ultimately, Saul's demise came not from David but from his hand during battle. This shows us that even though others may speak evil against us or seek our harm, their words and intentions do not have the final say. God's will prevail.

Lesson: They may manifest if you do not counter negative words spoken over your life. Just as Saul's words of harm did not materialize in David's life, so must we resist and counter any negative declarations.

3. The Warfare of Words

Words are part of spiritual warfare. Whether spoken out loud or harbored in people's imaginations, the enemy can use negative words to attack us. Ephesians 6:12 reminds us that our battle is not against flesh and blood but against spiritual forces. Therefore, we must learn how to counter these spiritual attacks.

A. Negative Expectations and Imagination

Sometimes, people don't have to speak negatively for spiritual warfare to occur. People may carry negative expectations or suspicions about you, which can also affect your spiritual atmosphere. In such cases, you must return these negative projections to the sender through prayer.

Evil Imagination: People can harbor evil imaginations or expect you to fail. If not addressed, these negative energies can manifest in your life. Satan uses these tactics to trap us. Be aware of the people who constantly expect you to stumble—they may be releasing negative energy against you, and it's essential to counter that energy with prayer and faith in God's promises.

B. Neutralizing Negative Words

When negative words are spoken against us, we must learn how to neutralize them. Isaiah 54:17 (KJV) says, "No weapon that is formed against thee shall prosper; and every tongue that shall rise against thee in judgment thou shalt condemn. This is the heritage of the servants of the LORD, and their righteousness is of me, saith the LORD."

David understood this. He never allowed himself to stay in a place of negativity or foolishness. When God rebuked him or corrected him, he immediately sought to align himself with wisdom and God's will.

4. The Authority of God's Word

The ultimate power to counter negative words is found in the

Word of God. The words spoken by others pale compared to the authority of God's Word.

A. *Declaring God's Word:*

When people speak against you, God's Word is the final authority. David declared, "But you, O Lord, are a shield around me, my glory, the One who lifts my head high" (Psalm 3:3, AMPC). This declaration of faith reminds us that God's Word is a shield that protects us from the arrows of negative words.

Just as a bird may fly over your head, you can prevent it from nesting, and so can we prevent negative words from taking root in our lives. By confessing God's Word and the authority of Scripture, we neutralize negative words, paralyze their power, and release God's blessing.

B. *The Covenant of God's Protection:*

As believers, we are under a covenant of protection. Psalm 91:4 tells us that God covers us with His feathers, and under His wings, we find refuge. No words of harm, no curses, and no negative imaginations can penetrate the protective shield that God provides.

We must stand in faith, declaring the Word of God over our lives, families, and futures.

5. *Glory, Honor, and Shekinah*

God's glory not only protects us from harm, but it also exalts us. When David declared that God was his glory, he placed the responsibility for his dignity, reputation, and success in God's hands.

A. *The Shekinah Glory*

The Shekinah, or the brilliant, manifest presence of God, is a spiritual reality and a source of our earthly strength. God's glory will bring us honor, respect, and the fulfillment of His promises. It is the essence of who He is, and through this glory, we are empowered to live victorious lives, free from the chains of negative words and curses.

Words are powerful, but God's word is more powerful than anything spoken against you. Whether through negative words, evil imaginations, or spiritual attacks, we have the authority through Christ to neutralize every force against us. As Psalm 3 reminds us, God is our shield and our glory. He lifts our heads high and causes us to walk in victory.

Let us commit today to being mindful of our words and countering every negative word with the truth of God's Word. As we do, we will walk in His glory, protected from harm and blessed beyond measure.

PART TWO: DEEPENING YOUR SPIRITUAL WALK

CHAPTER NINE

EMBRACING THE NEW THINGS GOD IS DOING

I stand here confidently now because this altar holds no failing life or destiny. You're not going to fail. God has a plan for your success, and I announce today that you, your family, and your future are freshly anointed with His presence. As we come together on this momentous occasion—the final day of May, a day set aside for a prophetic encounter—I want to talk about the fresh things God is bringing about in your life. With God, there are no coincidences—only divine appointments—and today is the start of a brand-new chapter in your life.

1. God is doing a new thing

"Behold, I will do a new thing; now it shall spring forth; shall you not know it?" proclaims God in Isaiah 43:19. I'll even create rivers in the desert and a path across the wild." God is telling you that you are going to experience new things. I want to reassure you that the devil cannot prevent you from moving on to the next chapter of your destiny as we enter this season. He won't be able to stop you from continuing if he can't stop you from being here.

In the name of Jesus, we announce today that every power, situation, and adversary that has attempted to undermine or sabotage God's purpose for your life is destroyed! I'm here to say that your expectations won't be dashed during this anticipated season (Proverbs 23:18). God is bringing you into a time when the seeds He has sown in your life will begin to show themselves to the outside world. God's new creations will be visible in your ministry, family, profession, and destiny, among other areas of your life.

2. Preparing the soil of your heart

However, as we embark on this season of change, we also need to recognize how crucial preparedness is. In Matthew 13:3–9, Jesus shares the parable of the sower to illustrate how the state of the soil affects a seed's ability to germinate and produce fruit. The seed stands for God's message, promises, and the fresh things He brings forth in your life. For these seeds to sprout, our hearts need to be rich soil, prepared to nurture and safeguard the seeds God is sowing.

God often gives us new things, but we cannot hold onto them. Why? Because we have not adequately cultivated the soil of our hearts. If we let the worries enter our shallow or rocky hearts of this world or the deceitfulness of riches choke the world, then the new things God is doing will not take root. Today, I declare over you that your heart will be fertile, free from the birds of the air that come to steal the seed and that your life will produce maximally in Jesus' name!

3. Recognize the New Things and Protect Them

It is vital to fight for their protection and acknowledge the new things that God is accomplishing. Because we failed to keep an eye on what God was doing, many of us have lost out on chances or rewards. We gave the new thing no opportunity to develop because we let life's stresses, persecutions, and challenges take it away. The rocks of disappointment and bitterness, the thorns of concern, and the sun of persecution may threaten the development of God's work in your life.

Like farmers who guard their crops from damage, we must be watchful. *"Break up your fallow ground, and do not sow among thorns,"* Jeremiah 4:3 commands. To truly grasp the essence of God, we must do, we must take action. This is not a time to be passive. We must remove the thorns—whether they are spiritual, emotional, or psychological warfare—that try to choke the new things God is birthing in us. The enemy will not have access to what God has planted in your life!

4. *Going Deep with God*

You must dive deep to encounter the magnificence God has in store for you. Shallow Christianity cannot sustain the fresh things God is doing. Your ability to withstand hardship will increase with the depth of your roots. The righteous person is compared to a tree planted by streams of water in Psalm 1:3, which bears fruit in season and whose leaf does not wither. No amount of hardship or persecution can pull you up when your roots are firmly planted in God.

Now is the time to become closer to God. Live a life characterized by prayer, fasting, and closeness to the Holy Spirit. I implore you to schedule some time for prayer, particularly around midnight when spiritual conflicts are most intense. Don't be shallow in your walk with God. Go deep, stay deep, and grow up strong in Him. Just like an acorn grows into a mighty oak tree, God is growing something mighty in your life that will last for generations.

5. *Understanding the Warfare*

Realize you are engaged in a spiritual war as you tend to defend the new things God is doing. The enemy is constantly looking to steal or corrupt the new things that God is creating. We need to be conscious of how our surroundings affect our spiritual lives. It's simple to think that everything will work out since we're doing everything correctly. However, we still need to be vigilant even when we follow all the appropriate procedures. The Bible alerts us to the reality of spiritual warfare and "thorns" and tells us that we must struggle to uphold God's work.

Thorns stand for emotional struggles, character defects in oneself, and the deceitfulness of wealth. The devil plants thorns as foes to hinder growth. But God has given us the tools to cut down and burn off every thorn in our lives. We fight with God's word, prayer, and the sword of the Spirit. Don't be afraid to fight for what

God is doing in your life. Recognize the warfare and be willing to engage in spiritual battles to protect your destiny.

6. *Staying Alert in Harvest*

Proverbs 10:5 says, *"He who gathers in summer is a wise son, but he who sleeps in harvest is a son who causes shame."* We are in a harvest season, and God calls you alert and active. Don't sleep when God is calling you to work. If you are multitalented, this is the time to use every gift, talent, and skill God has given you. Don't wait for the ample opportunities to come before you act. Start where you are, and watch God multiply your efforts.

If you are an artist, create! If you are a writer, write! If you are a musician, release your music! Whatever God has placed in your hands, use it for His glory. Don't let procrastination or fear hold you back. Now is the time to release the books, the songs, the businesses, and the ministries that God has placed within you. The world is waiting for what God has planted in your life, and it's time for you to take action.

As we come to the end of this sermon, I want you to remember how valuable the new things God is doing in your life are. These seedlings need to be nurtured, planted and kept safe. In this harvest time, go deep with God, contend with spiritual conflicts, and exercise caution. God is working in your life in a way that will become evident to everyone. I proclaim that what God has sown will endure for many generations and that your life will produce abundant fruit. Indeed!

CHAPTER TEN

WAITING ON
GOD'S TIMING

Waiting on God is one of the most important aspects of a believer's faith journey. It is a call to put our trust in His knowledge, intent, and method, even in the face of our inability to comprehend the waiting. The importance of waiting on God, His trials during the waiting season, and the ultimate reason for divine timing are all covered in this chapter. We explore how trust, obedience, and patience play a part when God asks us to wait, applying scriptural understanding and real-world examples.

The Trumpet's Sound on the 30th Midnight

Midnight is a crucial turning point in biblical and prophetic symbolism. A significant event, the conclusion of one season and the start of another is about to occur. The 30th midnight reference suggests that God's timing might not align with our expectations. It can stand for the point at which everything that has been postponed eventually materializes.

God frequently blasts the trumpet at "midnight" on our spiritual journeys, inviting His people to see what He has prepared in His own time. The trumpet's blast signals a divine change at this hour, a time of awakening when God fulfills His promises. But it will only be heard by those who have waited patiently and remained vigilant and heedful to His call.

In His parable of the ten virgins (Matthew 25:1–13), Jesus

discussed the importance of waiting, pointing out that only the prudent ones—those who had prepared and kept an eye out —entered the bridal feast. The message is unmistakable: even though we may not be able to predict the precise moment, we must continue to be watchful, ready for God's moment of intervention, and confident that we will see His glory when the time comes.

Waiting on God's Schedule (Genesis 22:12 TLB)

The angel commanded, *"Don't lay a hand on the boy,"* according to Genesis 22:12. *"I now know that you genuinely fear God, so please do not harm him in any way. Even your only kid, your son, has not been hidden from me by you."* This scripture refers to the crucial turning point in Abraham's life—the call to sacrifice Isaac. Abraham obeyed the command even though it didn't make sense; he waited on God. His desire to follow instructions was evidence of his faith.

Waiting on God's timetable in our life frequently feels like a test that puts our patience and trust to the test. Like Abraham, we may be asked to give up something that holds special meaning, like a dream, a piece of property, or even a family member. However, in these instances, God is not only assessing our compliance but also examining our hearts' alignment. During this time of waiting, what is God asking you to consider? Is He putting your perseverance, humility, or trust to the test?

Passivity is not what it means to wait on God. It's a moment of active faith when we keep believing, praying, and submitting to His will, knowing that His promises will pass at the appropriate time. It says in Isaiah 40:31, "But they that wait upon the Lord shall renew their strength; they shall mount up with wings as eagles; they shall run, and not be weary; and they shall walk, and not faint."

Here, we see the power of waiting; its grit, perseverance, and eventual triumph demonstrated. By staying on God's timetable, we may be sure that we will receive what He has intended for us rather than what we have hurriedly sought after.

God's Test: What Is He Checking in You?

When Abraham put Isaac to the test, he was not a newborn. He was probably a young man who knew what was going on. This was an assessment of Abraham's faith in God's promise and his readiness to offer Isaac. Even though Isaac fulfilled the terms of God's covenant with Abraham, Abraham was prepared to return Isaac to God. What was God making sure of? It was the core of faith that was unwavering and obedience.

God puts us to the test in similar ways throughout our lives. To test whether we trust Him more than the gifts He has bestowed upon us, He can ask us to lay down our Isaacs, which are the same things that stand in for His promises to us. Do you have more faith in the Giver or the Gift? Are you devoted to the One who made the promise or to the promise itself? God utilizes these probing, heart-wrenching questions to hone our moral fiber and make sure our priorities are in order.

Furthermore, while we wait and undergo testing, our logic frequently clashes with our faith. Faith asks us to trust beyond our comprehension, even while logic tells us what God is asking doesn't make sense. We cross over into the world of divine possibilities when we put aside reason and establish a connection with the Spirit. In 1 Corinthians 2:9, the apostle Paul stated, "No eye has seen, no ear has heard, and no mind has imagined what God has prepared for those who love Him."

The Dangers of Rushing Ahead

Psalm 20:9 (MSG) reminds us to "*make the king a winner, God; the day we call, give us your answer.*" Although God wants us to succeed, there is a divine timeliness to the victory. We put ourselves in unneeded risk and spiritual peril when we rush ahead of God's plan. "*That which exposes your greatness and glory to worms is being flushed out in the name of Jesus,*" the passage warns.

If we try to accomplish our destiny before God's designated time, we can compromise the same rewards we are pursuing. Although the word "worms" is a metaphor for corruption, arrogance, and distraction, God wants us to succeed and does not want our accomplishments undermined. Instead, He desires that we maintain our prosperity while remaining modest and dependent on Him. Rushing God's work leads to disappointment, tiredness, and missed opportunities.

We must exercise caution to avoid working for the incorrect objectives to let these "worms" in and call into question the legitimacy of our accomplishments. God's instruction to wait also prevents us from being exposed to conflicts too soon for us to handle.

Supernatural Help in Waiting

The knowledge that we are not alone is among our most consoling assurances while we wait on God. "*May Yahweh answer you in your day of trouble,*" says Psalm 20:1-2 (TPT). May you be protected from all evil in the name of Jacob's God. May His refuge send out miraculous assistance."

God provides us with divine support during times of waiting. This support could take the form of heavenly power, defense, supply, or even opportune inspiration from His word or others. We have to have faith that God is coordinating everything according to His plan while we wait. When the time comes, there will be no denying His assistance and the breakthrough.

Waiting is a season of preparation rather than passivity. God shapes us for the future He has planned during these silent, seemingly unhurried times. He clears the air, sharpens our intentions, and fortifies our faith. Not only is the promise fulfilled when these seasons end, but we also have a greater appreciation for God's faithfulness and a heart that is committed to Him.

Trusting the Process

All things considered, waiting on God is a disciplined spiritual practice that includes faith, endurance, and confidence. While we wait, we learn to surrender control over the timing and course of our lives and align our hearts with God's goals. We might find solace in knowing that God has a perfect plan and knows when to act.

We must be unwavering in our belief that God's timing is always ideal, regardless of the time of day—whether at midnight when the trumpet sounds or during peaceful introspection. We know He will provide us with safety, supernatural assistance, and ultimate fulfillment of His promises while we await Him. Our loyalty, faith, and hard work will not go unappreciated in these times—instead, they will be rewarded in ways that surpass our wildest expectations.

CHAPTER ELEVEN

DEDICATION TO
THE SPIRIT

Devotion on the path of faith is more than just pledging; it is a complete surrender of our will to God's divine plan. This dedication shapes our spiritual lives, which affects how we communicate with God and follow His instructions. We must put God's will above our own to dedicate ourselves to Him, believing He knows what is best for us.

Thinking back on my personal experiences, I can't help but think of a crucial period in the second quarter of this year. It was a period of unstable finances and difficult personal times. The idea of "financial seed sowing," in which a person offers some of their earnings as a gesture of faith, is well known. In my instance, I donated every penny I owned to my bishop's ministry as a seed. This gesture, represented by *"horses and chariots"* (Psalm 20:7), was a proclamation of trust in God rather than reliance on secular systems. It was not only about providing money. This was a pledge to await God's supply and timing.

On the 30th, at midnight, we gathered for a special ceremony, hoping to have spiritual contact. The sound of the trumpet resonated in my spirit at that very instant, and I felt the Holy Spirit moving among us. It was an appeal to understand the significance of waiting according to God's timing, as stated in Genesis 22:12 (TLB) when God put Abraham's loyalty and trust to the test. *"What does God know about you, and what is He approving in you?"* was the question that began to arise in my heart.

Giving Up Reason to Follow the Spirit

Waiting on God takes determination and frequently defies logic and comprehension. Think about the narrative of Abraham and Isaac. Abraham was a man of tremendous faith and experience; he was no longer a novice. However, God put his devotion to the test when he asked him to sacrifice his son, Isaac, who was a young man rather than a kid. God was probing Abraham's heart to see if he would put aside reason to follow an order that went against common sense.

We frequently encounter circumstances where we must put aside logic to follow the Spirit's guidance. It's simple to get sucked into the struggle between our feelings and wits. True dedication, however, necessitates putting aside reason in favor of spiritual connection. We risk missing the benefits that lie ahead once we obey God when we put our understanding ahead of His direction.

False ideas and teachings will deceive many, even the elect, as Matthew 24:24 (TLB) forewarns. As a result, it is crucial to remain rooted in the Bible's truth and seek direction from the Holy Spirit. We must set aside time for prayer, reading the Bible, and hearing from the Spirit. God can renew and change our thoughts when we give Him our hearts.

In my perspective, giving my money to God as a seed was a spiritual act that called for total trust in Him rather than just a financial transaction. It served as a reminder that the Lord is the source of my assistance (Psalm 20:9 MSG). By putting my faith in God and putting aside my logic, I made room for His miraculous help.

The Blessing of Supernatural Help

Acknowledging that we are not alone in our challenges is another dedication aspect. God wants to bring assistance into our lives. At that midnight prayer meeting, I said we would receive supernatural support from the sanctuary to help us win our battles. Spiritual battles carry a great price, and we frequently find ourselves in predicaments that call for divine assistance. It is critical to recognize that when we commit to God's plan, aid is accessible.

"*That which exposes your greatness and glory to worms is being flushed out in the name of Jesus,*" I declared among difficulties. This statement addresses the spiritual truth that the adversary frequently tries to undo our successes. The worms represent what would devour our victories and transform them into defeats. God wants us to win, but in order to do so, we need to be watchful and aggressive in our spiritual lives.

Psalm 20:1-2 (TPT) is a reminder from the psalmist that the Lord will assist when we are in need. When we commit our lives to God, we can depend on Him to meet our needs. Knowing that God is our supplier and protector, we must rely on God's Word's authority when dealing with legal disputes, money problems, or health emergencies.

I prayed for you that "every wicked worm assigned to reproach you, be burnt." This stirring declaration reminds us that we are powerful because of Christ. Because we believe that God is our sanctuary and that His Word is accurate, we can declare victory over every obstacle. Divine protection and aid are made possible by our unwavering allegiance to Him.

The Importance of Spiritual Protocol

Comprehending the relevance of spiritual protocols is vital. Even though we all make mistakes in our relationship with God, going against spiritual protocol can have dire repercussions. Following spiritual procedures allows God to work in our lives in predictable ways and brings His power and presence into our situations.

While I have made mistakes, I have always tried to follow spiritual rules to the letter. For example, it is essential to approach God with a heart of repentance, humility, and dedication while asking for His assistance. When we approach Him in faith and obedience, we align with God's purposes for our lives.

Every one of us has to struggle against the powers of evil from time to time in spiritual combat. We must remember that we are sent helpers in these conflicts. Not only are we the ones who receive assistance, but we are also the means by which God can aid others. When we give ourselves to Him, we become vehicles for His love and peace.

The Unfortunate Case of Jonah

The purpose of Jonah's story is to teach dedication. God sent Jonah to the Ninevites to deliver a message, but Jonah chose to elude his mission. As we can see in Jonah 1:1 (TLB), God spoke to Jonah, but he declined the invitation. His journey put him in unfortunate circumstances that ultimately led to his regret.

The story of Jonah reminds us of the importance of diligently responding to God's call. Amittai, which means "truth," is a reflection of Jonah's lineage; nevertheless, he rejected the truth that God was trying to teach him during his life. In the biblical account, he turned out not to be a loyal servant but a question mark.

Sadly, many of us are strong enough to fight on our father's side, but we have problems with our mother's side. Spiritual influences from our upbringing may interfere with our commitment to God.

Addressing the Worms Within

All in all, we must be aware of the worms and spiritual obstructions we might harbor within. They can undermine our commitment to God's purpose and appear as dread, uncertainty, or insecurity. With the help of the Holy Spirit, we can take on these problems head-on.

In Jesus' name, I ask that everything that may have come from your mother's side and turned into a worm in your spirit be stopped. God wants us to live victorious lives, free from the weights that bind us. If we are committed to the Spirit and the authority of God's Word, we can overcome every challenge and live in the fullness of God's promises.

May we commit our thoughts and emotions to the Lord, putting our faith in His providence and timing. As we wait for His schedule, we can rest assured that He orchestrates everything for our benefit. We will experience His supernatural assistance through our commitment and grow closer to Him.

Ultimately, devotion is a lifelong process of surrender, confidence, and trust in the God who asks us to be more than conquerors in Christ Jesus. It is not a one-time occurrence. Let us remain steadfast in the knowledge that our commitment to the Spirit will pay off through blessings and successes.

CHAPTER TWELVE

SPIRITUAL PROTOCOLS AND HELP

F ollowing divine instructions is a compass in our spiritual journey, enabling us to face life's challenges with confidence and trust. This chapter will discuss the importance of following spiritual guidelines and the connection between believing in God for help and being a sent helper. This session will explore the essence of dedication to the Spirit and show how a heart aligned with God can produce supernatural support through scripture, personal experiences, and prophetic announcements.

Upholding Spiritual Protocols (Matthew 24:24 TLB)

Believers need to comprehend and follow spiritual etiquette. "For false Christs and false prophets will rise and perform great miracles and wonders to deceive, if possible, even God's chosen ones," according to Matthew 24:24 (TLB). This verse calls us to be rooted in our faith and the integrity of God's Word while highlighting the importance of discernment. Spiritual protocols are heavenly instructions, not just rules, that keep us safe from deceit and point us toward our divine destiny.

Maintaining these procedures calls for intentionality. It entails developing a mind that aligns with God's teachings and a heart that seeks God sincerely. Devotion to spiritual concerns frequently requires us to put aside reason and put our faith in the unknown. This can be difficult, mainly when our environment depends too much on material fixes. But regardless of our circumstances, God calls us to a higher standard of faith—a faith that is based on believing in His promises.

I can think of a personal story that exemplifies this idea. I once experienced severe financial difficulties and felt compelled to plant a seed in the ministry. I had many worries about my capacity to make ends meet, so I had to suspend my logic to do this act of faith. Still, I took all I owned and planted it as a seed. By doing this, I practiced a spiritual routine that demonstrated my faith in God rather than in material solutions, not just a financial transaction.

The tricky part is giving yourself over to God's direction. When we commit to Him, our emotions must guide us even though our minds may struggle with our choices. This heart-centered strategy is essential because it synchronizes our goals with God's life plan. We get into trouble when our hearts and our reasoning don't agree. Nonetheless, we can confidently face life's obstacles if we intentionally set aside our logic and establish a heart-to-heart communication with the Spirit.

Relying on God for Assistance (MSG, Psalm 20:9)

Following spiritual protocol, we must acknowledge that we are sent assistants in God's kingdom. *"Give victory to our king, O God, the day we call on you,"* says Psalm 20:9 (MSG). This scripture emphasizes how crucial it is to ask God for assistance and have faith that He will answer. When we commit ourselves to God's work, we open up channels for other people to receive His help.

Being a sent helper entails reaching out to people in need and asking for help for ourselves. This dual function strengthens our faith and enhances our spiritual lives. Our actions of faith-based compassion have a cascading impact that improves the lives of those we assist and transforms and heals our own.

God wants us to succeed, but He doesn't want us to achieve success just for the sake of success. We must strive for triumphs that exalt Him and bring about enduring transformation. The idea of "working out" what makes us great is a powerful reminder that the things that want to ruin us shouldn't overshadow our triumphs (Psalm 20:1-2 TPT). Put another way, we must guard our gifts and ensure spiritual deterioration doesn't undermine them.

We might say, "I command supernatural help to be sent to you," as we trust God. This statement is an affirmation based on the authority of God's Word, not just a wish. It is an expression of faith that acknowledges the influence of supernatural help in our lives. We can believe that assistance is coming when we encounter difficulties in our relationships, finances, or health.

Dedication to the Spirit

Becoming dedicated to the Spirit is more than just following a routine. We must connect our hearts with His desires to enable God to act through us. Deep insight into this dedication may be found in Genesis 22:12 (TLB), which asks us what God knows about us and what He values in us. The narrative of Abraham and Isaac is a potent warning about the extent to which God is willing to try our faith. God didn't ask Abraham to sacrifice Isaac because He needed a sacrifice; instead, He did it to show Abraham's true nature, which is one of faith and obedience.

Isaac was a young man who could comprehend the ramifications of what was happening; he was not a baby. God was testing Abraham's level of faith. God examines our commitment to Him and our hearts in the same spirit. Are we prepared to give up our goals, plans, and desires to follow His? Allowing our hearts to direct our acts even when our logic finds them difficult to understand is the core of being devoted to the Spirit.

People may think we are "suspending our brains" when we adopt this degree of commitment. This is an appeal to value spiritual insight over logical reasoning, not a demand to give up intellect. The struggle with faith frequently occurs in the mind, where worries and uncertainties can impair our judgment. Thus, we must deliberately follow our hearts when presented with a choice that aligns with God's will.

The Power of Prayer and Declarations

Prayer is vital to following spiritual guidelines and asking God for assistance. Our prayers are expressions of our faith in God's power to step in and help us, in addition to being requests for help. When we pray, we open the door between heaven and earth and allow the supernatural to intervene in our everyday lives.

In the face of daunting obstacles, I frequently find myself praying fervently. I say, "I plead the blood of Jesus over my situation" during these times. Jesus' blood has more power than Abel's and speaks of more incredible things. It addresses our destinies, our families, and our callings. We find courage and confidence in our proclamations, knowing that even in the darkest moments, God is at work.

I frequently emphasize the need for mercy in my prayers for myself and the people around me. God has great power when it comes to mercy. We can confidently approach His throne because we know His grace is sufficient to cover our transgressions. Since we all need God's grace, we must be willing to show kindness to others to seek His help.

The path of spiritual devotion and obedience to divine laws is a joint undertaking between the individual and the community. Let us remember that we are not alone while negotiating life's difficulties. We are called to be sent assistants as we rely on God to provide the support we require to overcome our challenges. We must not waver in our resolve to respect spiritual customs, appreciating the significance of discernment and faith.

As Jonah suffered the consequences of his disobedience, so must we endeavor to live devoted lives in submission to God. Regardless of the obstacles our paternal or maternal lineage may have left behind, we can thwart any evil force attempting to impede our advancement using the power of the Holy Spirit. As we align our hearts with His purpose, we will enjoy the fruits of a life devoted to God and the fullness of His assistance.

May we never waver from the authority of God's Word and put our faith in His omnipotent assistance, knowing that our commitment to Him unlocks a world of blessings beyond our comprehension. Putting Christ as the center of our triumph and glory, let us diligently pray, faith, and deeds, knowing that our lives will bear these emblems.

CHAPTER THIRTEEN

BATTLES AND
DELIVERANCE

We frequently encounter conflicts on the path of faith that have the potential to stop us in our tracks. These conflicts are not just material or physical; they often take on spiritual dimensions. The metaphors "worms" and "darkness" refer to the unseen forces that work to destroy our achievements. We are reminded of the necessity of divine intervention in these problems by Psalm 20:1-2 (TPT): "May the Lord answer you in your day of difficulty! May you feel safe with the God of Jacob! May he provide you with support from Zion and assistance from the sanctuary!

We have exceptional prospects throughout the year's second quarter, particularly in light of our financial circumstances. Around this period, many people deal with heavy pressures, most of which are associated with seemingly unpayable debt. I can recall an instance in which I was in this circumstance. I boldly decided to donate my remaining funds to the ministry as a seed, taking a risk. It was a choice based on faith—faith that God would supply. This conduct was motivated more by a desire to show my faith than fear and to line my actions up with my conviction that God can intervene rather than the money itself.

We show absolute reliance when we trust in God instead of human institutions. Thinking about this, we have to ask ourselves: Do we trust in the name of our God, or do we rely on "horses and chariots"? It is essential to ask this question since it highlights our spiritual protocols. We must put our faith in God as the ultimate support provider and connect our hearts with His objectives.

Understanding that God is constantly assessing our loyalty while we fight these conflicts is critical. This is aptly demonstrated in Genesis 22:12 (TLB): *"Refrain from touching the boy! I know that you genuinely fear God, so please don't harm him in any way. You haven't kept anything from me, not even your one and only son."*

God tests Abraham's faith in this narrative, showing how struggles frequently present opportunities for personal development and assurance of loyalty. What about us does God approve of through our struggles? What does He see when He looks into our souls during these trying times?

During this exam, Isaac wasn't just a kid; he was old enough to comprehend the consequences of what was going on. God evaluates our character based on the state of our hearts, not only the things we do on the outside. This brings us to a crucial point: rather than being a duty, our devotion to God should come from a deep-seated conviction.

Winning Without Worms Eating Your Victory

We must guard against the "worms" eating our victories as we pursue victory. Psalm 20:1-2 (TPT) highlights this fight against these forces of destruction. It serves as a reminder that even when we succeed, spiritual forces frequently work to thwart our achievements. We cannot toil tirelessly and then watch as those who wish to destroy us consume the triumphs we have worked so hard to achieve.

Maintaining spiritual customs in our lives is essential. These are the rules and directives that God has given us in Scripture to help us navigate these conflicts. Matthew 24:24 (TLB) cautions against believing false prophets and messiahs who claim to be able to do unique marvels to trick even God's chosen people. Respecting these spiritual guidelines entails being aware of the lies around us and choosing to follow God's truth instead of the false impressions that try to seep into our hearts and minds.

When logic gets in the way of the heart's desires, many individuals are lost in a maze of uncertainty and disarray. God frequently speaks to us via our hearts, where His Spirit reveals the truth beyond our comprehension. We experience spiritual upheaval when our hearts and brains start to disagree. Sometimes, we must put aside reason to allow our hearts to commune with the Spirit. This link will enable us to overcome the limitations of reasoning that occasionally undermine our trust.

Though I have erred, the truth is that I have never purposefully broken spiritual rules. Every stumble is a warning to keep working hard and paying attention in our spiritual lives. To trust God for assistance, we must place ourselves in His kingdom as "sent helpers," prepared to give and receive supernatural assistance (Psalm 20:9 MSG).

We take a strong stance against the powers that want to harm us when we say, "That which exposes your greatness and glory to worms is being flushed out in the name of Jesus. We must demand in our fervent prayers that every worm and evil spirit be destroyed. We must declare war on the attacks on our lives, whether disease, financial difficulties, or interpersonal conflict.

I steadfastly assert the authority of God's Word in these struggles and demand the appearance of divine assistance. "I curse the worms, the darkness, and the spirit of death. I curse the cancer in your body. "Die by fire, worms, darkness, and rebellion!" We must use the force of our words to speak life and victory over any region that seems to be under attack.

The sanctuary's pledge of support is more than just a symbolic declaration; it signifies a tangible link to God's supply. By coming to the refuge for assistance, we connect with supernatural resources beyond our comprehension and not just seek out support from this world. This support can come in many forms, assisting us in overcoming our spiritual, emotional, and physical challenges.

We need to deal with the "wicked worms" that are meant to drag us down when we take stock of our lives. "I declare that every evil worm sent to bring you reproach is destroyed by fire." We can't afford to allow our successes to remain undefended. Every victory we have should be protected from the enemy's attempts to impede our advancement. Knowing God is at our side in every conflict, we must approach our struggles with purpose and clarity.

The "worms" that may have settled in our lives should be kept in mind as we go through these spiritual waters, particularly those rooted in maternal influences. In the name of Jesus, I pray for the Holy Spirit to stop whatever has come from your mother's side that is impeding your growth.

We are waging a spiritual war calling us to be watchful and proactive rather than only against flesh and blood. Let's sever the bonds of evil and ensure the forces trying to undo our successes don't taint them. We can triumph and attain genuine release through observance of spiritual guidelines, faith in God's assistance, and proactive participation in the conflict.

CHAPTER FOURTEEN

COMMANDING SUPERNATURAL HELP

We are reminded that the second quarter can be crucial for starting over in this season of divine potential. It's a time to pause, let go, and take back what is rightfully ours. God is calling us to act in faith during this time, to put our faith in His promises, and to show that He is the one we trust the most. I still remember a turning point when I made a leap of faith that altered how I perceived God's providence and omnipotence.

I decided to give my bishop the money I had received as a seed for my ministry. I was deciding to give up what I saw as my security was not easy. However, God was probing my heart to know if I would put my faith in the name of my God or horses and chariots. This question struck a deep chord with me. Although it appeared to be a financial choice initially, it was a test of spiritual loyalty. I decided to put my faith in God, give up on my temporary security, and invest in something enduring.

Many of you will witness firsthand the validation of what I have been teaching you on divine intervention and timing as the 30th draws closer to midnight. It involves more than just waiting; it involves actively anticipating God's divine intervention.

Genesis 22:12 (TLB) reminds us that God watches our actions and faith. When He looks into your heart, what does He see? What is in you does He approve of?

Think about Isaac, who was an adult when Abraham was asked

to sacrifice him rather than a toddler. The deed is under question, and Abraham's faith in God is as well. God was examining Abraham's willingness to offer up his only son as a sacrifice. God often uses our life to test our willingness to give up our "Isaacs."

Our spiritual journey demands a specific determination that calls for us to set aside reason and establish a close relationship with the Spirit. If we let our knowledge precede our faith, we risk not reaping God's benefits. Matthew 24:24 (TLB) cautions us of the possibility of deceit in the last days. We must avoid being sidetracked by diversions and stay grounded in the truth.

I firmly assert that God's Word is infallible and declare that a new chapter is beginning in your life. Psalm 20:9 (MSG) clarifies that anyone who trusts the Lord will receive divine assistance. God is not only calling you to win, but He also promises that in the name of Jesus, every demonic force and every worm that tries to eat your victory is being driven out.

Worms gnawing away at our wins is a powerful image. God wants you to grow and bloom like a palm tree, but not to the point where worms take over your accomplishments. You must ensure your prosperity is protected from spiritual bugs that could undo your hard work when you strive so hard for it. God wants you to triumph ultimately, free from the influence of evil or disobedience.

I fervently demand that you be sent magical assistance! I curse death, the spirit of death, and whatever hidden evil or disobedience that may be present in your body. I proclaim that the Holy Spirit's fire consumes every evil worm sent to impede your advancement. Now is the time to summon your heavenly help from the sanctuary, where angels are sent to defend you.

While we pray, we must be precise. You need to confront every spirit of rebellion causing chaos in your life. In your life, I pray for mercy and that God will intervene in every seemingly hopeless legal, financial, and employment circumstance. All the sour heat that recklessness and folly produce will be converted into divine favor. I pray the blood of Jesus over your circumstances because it speaks a better language than Abel's. Our defense, our shield, and the source of our victory is the blood of Jesus.

May the blood of Jesus cover your family, calling, and destiny. Let the blood assist you in sorting through the mess and uncertainty surrounding the decisions you are now digesting. May the Lord make you victorious and send you assistance from Zion. I want you to picture God's protection surrounding you like a fortress and ensure that nothing wrong can ever enter your life while I release this prayer.

I pray that the Holy Spirit can stop any demonic influence from your family as we come to the end of this chapter. In the name of Jesus, I announce that any worms of discontent, stagnation, or rebellion rooted from your mother's side in your life are defeated. May you triumph over the past, break free from its bonds, and enter the new season God has planned for you with courage.

The Lord is our stronghold, and He will ensure that we have the supernatural power and support to overcome every obstacle. Remember, it is in relinquishing our minds and believing God that we gain true strength. Accept who you are—a conqueror, a victor, and a child of the Most High. God. The battle is not yours; it belongs to the Lord.

CHAPTER FIFTEEN

MERCY AND THE BLOOD OF JESUS

Mercy is a profound and transforming principle deeply woven into the fabric of our relationship with God in the giant narrative of our faith. Jesus' blood is a potent symbol of that mercy, a source of deliverance, and a shield. This chapter will examine the significance of expressing mercy over irresponsibility and stupidity and appealing to the blood of Jesus for protection and deliverance.

Pleading the Blood for Protection and Deliverance

More than just a symbol, the blood of Jesus provides us with heavenly assurance that keeps us safe during our darkest moments. The sacrificial act of Christ on the cross, which represents our salvation, redemption, and victory over sin and death, is invoked as we pray for the blood. ***"And they defeated him by the blood of the Lamb and by their testimony,"* according to Revelation 12:11 (TLB).** This verse emphasizes how blood can defeat evil and give us the upper hand against our enemies.

As we go through life, we must become aware of the spiritual conflicts around us. We often encounter circumstances that leave us feeling overburdened, whether related to debt, health issues, or interpersonal disputes. We must appeal for divine intervention in these trying times by lifting the blood of Jesus.

In my life, there was a time when debt hung heavy over me like a cloud. I felt imprisoned and under a lot of strain. But it brought to mind the importance of planting seeds of trust. I used the rest of my money for the ministry as a seed donation. The knowledge that God wants to see if we rely on His supply rather than our resources drove this deed, not desperation. **We are reminded in Psalm 20:9 (MSG) to** *"Give victory to our king, O God, and answer our cry for help."*

God wishes occasionally to test our faith. By midnight on the 30th, I was convinced many people would see the reality of these teachings. I had to trust that the Lord had a great purpose for my life at this particular moment and wait upon Him. As Genesis 22:12 (TLB) demonstrated, *"Don't touch the boy! As long as you don't harm him, I will know that you genuinely fear God. You haven't kept anything from me, not even your one and only son."* Here, God, like Abraham and Isaac, looks into our hearts to discover how far we are willing to trust Him.

To adequately plead Jesus' blood, we must take a specific spiritual stance. We must put aside our rational minds and immerse our hearts in faith. *"Because false messiahs and false prophets will rise and perform great wonders and miracles to deceive, if possible, even God's chosen ones,"* as Matthew 24:24 (TLB) forewarns us. Rather than letting our understanding dictate our actions, we must remain watchful and ensure that our hearts align with God's plan.

Declaring Mercy Over Carelessness and Foolishness

Although we think of mercy as something we should seek, it is equally necessary to announce mercy over our own lives and grant it to others, especially in the face of stupidity and negligence. We all experience times of weakness; we depend on God's grace to get through them.

By pleading for compassion, we admit our sinfulness and dependence on God's kindness. It is simple to become careless in the middle of chaos and make choices that can divert us from God's plan. However, we may change our situation if we confess Jesus' kindness and beg for His blood.

I can recall a period when I made reckless choices and

relationships, believing that there were no repercussions for what I did. But, I had a significant change due to prayer and the blood's plea. I saw that God's mercy was an active power that brought about repair rather than only a safety net. We discover His mercy may cover our carelessness when approaching the throne of grace.

James 2:13 says, *"Mercy triumphs over judgment"* (NIV). We are voicing our strong faith by pleading for pity over our folly. We must never forget that God's mercy is ever-present, prepared to forgive us of our transgressions and provide us with the tools we need to succeed.

We must never lose sight of the fact that Jesus' blood can atone for our transgressions, even when we feel overcome by them. We recognize the sufficiency of His grace while we confess our failings. The blood acts as a spokesperson for us, ensuring that our identity as God's loving children, rather than our history, defines us.

We also need to show this mercy to people close to us. In our communities, families, and places of employment, we must provide mercy when things appear hopeless. This entails realizing that recklessness and stupidity may also affect other people. When we face these circumstances with a merciful heart, we enable the blood of Jesus to restore and cure everyone we come into contact with.

The Importance of Spiritual Protocol

Following spiritual guidelines is essential for navigating our spiritual journey. The core of our faith is found in our commitment to God and the authority of His word, even if we are human and may stumble and make mistakes. I have learned the value of abiding by God's divine order, yet I have never purposefully broken spiritual etiquette.

We also become sent helpers by trusting God to provide extraterrestrial assistance. **"May the Lord be your shelter in your day of danger,"** says Psalm 20:1-2 (TPT). May Jacob's God protect you from all evil. This verse serves as a reminder that when we follow God's instructions, we put ourselves in a position to receive divine support.

Furthermore, it's critical to comprehend how our decisions affect our spiritual selves. In the name of Jesus, we must declare that everything that puts our greatness at risk is being eliminated. Spiritual parasites shouldn't be allowed to devour our victories in the religious journey. God wants us to succeed—not just on this globe but hereafter.

We use the power of Jesus' blood to triumph over disease, disobedience, and other spiritual obstacles. We must courageously approach the throne and ask for heavenly help in all our lives—financially, professionally, and health-wise.

Let us continue to be watchful as we travel together in faith, confessing forgiveness for ourselves and others and abiding by the spiritual rules that direct us. Let us plead the blood of Jesus. By doing this, we set ourselves up for a life full of God's mercy, grace, protection, and deliverance. Indeed.

CHAPTER SIXTEEN

THE WISDOM OF PRIORITIZATION IN OUR LIVES

Proverbs 10:1 (TPT) states, "A wise son brings joy to his father, but a foolish son brings grief to his mother." This verse captures the significance of discernment and setting priorities in our lives, especially for parents.

Foolishness is not knowing how to prioritize life and recognize what is essential. Raising intelligent children who understand how to concentrate their lives on what is necessary should be the ultimate ambition of a mother—and, in fact, any parent.

The Role of Wisdom in Parenting

Fathers can instruct and bestow blessings on their kids, but if those sons are foolish, the father's teachings and benefits might be for naught, and the mother would suffer. Think about Abigail's tale in 1 Samuel 25. Although Abigail was a knowledgeable woman, she found it challenging to successfully teach her boys the lessons she had learned. This teaches us an important lesson: wisdom needs to be sought out and shared.

We cannot undervalue the importance of instilling wisdom in our children, especially in a society that frequently prizes intelligence above wisdom. Wisdom is the cornerstone of a successful existence. It shapes our decisions, our habits, and our relationships. As parents, we must ensure that our children develop their judgment and know what is essential.

The Divine Gift of the Earth

When God created the earth, He rented it to the first creation. But when He created man, He gave humanity the title deed to the world. This vital realization emphasizes our duty as God's stewards of his creation. We weren't just handed the earth; it was entrusted to us.

God eradicated the former occupants of the earth—often referred to as "aliens"—when He expelled them. It took millions of years for humanity to evolve. However, the ownership deed still belonged to humanity when it came time to exterminate man from the planet for his disobedience. This is crucial because it illustrates the legal conflict between Satan and humanity.

"*Those who don't believe have had their minds blinded by Satan, the god of this evil world,*" according to 2 Corinthians 4:4 (TLB). This text reminds us that by disobedience, Satan was able to take the title deed from man legitimately. After eating from the forbidden tree, Adam and Eve gave the title deed to the one they obeyed, according to Genesis 3:7 (TLB). An important turning point in human history was this transfer.

The Coming of Jesus

We have to understand the significance of Jesus' arrival in this situation. Because only men could reclaim the planet, Christ came as a man. The plan of redemption was put into action to make up for what was lost. According to Matthew 4:8 (TLB) and Luke 4:5 (TLB), Satan tempted Jesus with the kingdoms of the world, and since Jesus did not rebuke him, it was implied that at that point, Satan's claim was legitimate.

This hypothetical situation is a potent reminder of the risks associated with our decisions. The term "only" was a cunning deception tactic used by Satan. He made God's commandments seem difficult and trivialized their significance, making his solutions seem enticing and straightforward. We are still affected by this deceit in our daily lives.

God's Collaboration Against Darkness

God made people believe we would work with Him to drive out evil. The introduction of darkness came about as a result of disobedience; it was not intended. As a result, we must prioritize the correct things in our lives and live by God's wisdom and will.

Breaking the rules in a game is embarrassing for a man, and the same is true in real life. Even while we could dismiss certain things as unimportant, they frequently cause many people to unfulfilled their potential. Wisdom assists us in maintaining focus on our mission and calling in a world full of distractions.

The Call to Greatness

In Genesis 12:1-3 (TLB), we find God's call to Abraham: "*Leave your country, your people, and your father's household and go to the land I will show you.*" This was a call to greatness, prioritizing God's plan over personal comfort and familiarity. God promised Abraham that he would be a great nation and that all earthly families would be blessed through him. This call was not merely for Abraham but for all of us to embrace our destiny and prioritize our obedience to God.

Understanding Prioritization

To prioritize effectively, we must discern what truly matters. This means setting aside our desires, fears, and doubts to focus on God's purpose for our lives. It requires wisdom to recognize the distractions that keep us from living fully in our calling. Our journey is not just about us but about how our lives can glorify God and impact those around us.

Living with Purpose and Intention

As we move forward, let us commit to living with intention. Let us seek wisdom daily, understanding that it is a precious gift. When prioritizing our relationship with God, we open ourselves to His guidance and direction. This means spending time in His Word, seeking His presence in prayer, and being receptive to His voice.

Moreover, we must model this wisdom for our children and those around us. Our actions speak louder than words. By living wisely, we demonstrate the importance of prioritization and its impact on our lives and the lives of others.

CONCLUSION

Every believer has a priceless opportunity to assess, realign, and renew their lives and walk with God and spiritual commitments, just as we stated at the beginning. This is the moment to reset, to concentrate once more on obedience, powerful prayers, and faith that can stifle the enemy's plots.

A.W. Tozer wisely noted, *"God is looking for those with whom He can do the impossible—what a pity we plan only the things we can do by ourselves."* Putting your trust in God opens the door to a life filled with His fullness and the unthinkable.

Even in the face of life's difficulties and obstacles, every Christian is encouraged to reiterate their faith in God's omnipotence, to go beyond words, and to embrace a greater confidence in His providence.

God is not interested in having a surface-level, fleeting connection with us. He is looking for a natural, profound path that changes our lives. It is the responsibility of the modern believer to awaken their faith in the same way as the ancient patriarchs—those who believed God unquestioningly and obeyed His voice even when the way was unclear.

When we walk closely with God, we choose what is most valuable and enduring. We position ourselves to reject lukewarmness and focus on eternal matters. This is the key to maximizing heavenly treasures. Consider the rich young ruler—had he followed Jesus, he would have gained far more than his wealth could ever offer.

C.S. Lewis once said, *"Aim at heaven, and you will get earth thrown in. Aim at earth, and you will get neither."*

Therefore, don't overlook the essential things: advancing God's kingdom, gaining souls for Christ, and accumulating wealth in paradise. May God's faithfulness envelop you as you enter this new season of commitment, understanding, and supernatural assistance. Have faith in Him, and may you never come up short in pursuing His everlasting plan.

A SPECIAL CALL TO SALVATION & NEW BEGINNINGS FROM APOSTLE DR. DAVID PHILEMON

Dear Beloved,

God loves you deeply and has brought you to this moment for a reason. No matter your past, His love and forgiveness are available to you.

The Bible says in John 3:16, "For God so loved the world that He gave His one and only Son, that whoever believes in Him shall not perish but have eternal life." Jesus Christ came to save you, offering you a new life of purpose and peace.

If you're ready to accept Jesus as your Lord and Savior, pray this simple prayer:

The Salvation Prayer

"Heavenly Father, I come to You in the Name of Jesus. I acknowledge that I am a sinner in need of a Savior. I believe that Jesus Christ is Your Son, that He died for my sins, and that You raised Him from the dead. I repent of my sins and turn to You with my

Whole heart. Jesus, I ask You to come into my life. Be my Lord and my Savior. I surrender my life to You. Fill me with Your Holy Spirit, guide me on the path of righteousness, and help me to follow Your script for my life. Thank you, Father, for saving me. In the name of Jesus. Amen."

Welcome to the Family of God!

If you have just prayed this prayer, Congratulations! You are now a child of God, and heaven is rejoicing. Your journey has begun, and we're here to support you as you grow in faith and discover God's unique plans for you.

Next Steps:
• Connect with a Bible-believing church.
• Read the Bible Daily: God's Word is your guide.
• Pray Regularly: Prayer is your lifeline to God.
• Share Your Faith: Don't keep the good news to yourself.

www.ingramcontent.com/pod-product-compliance
Lightning Source LLC
Chambersburg PA
CBHW071904020426
42331CB00010B/2661